C000300680

DAVID GOOD]

BLITZ REQUIEM

WORDS BY

FRANCIS WARNER

VOCAL SCORE

COLIN SMYTHE LTD

2014

Published 2014 by Colin Smythe Limited
38 Mill Lane, Gerrards Cross, Buckinghamshire, SL9 8BA

who also publishes *Six Anthems* by David Goode and Francis Warner
together with a CD of these anthems sung by the choir of King's College, Cambridge,
conducted by Stephen Cleobury during chapel services.

The publisher wishes to thank the Steven and Michael Latner families
for a generous grant towards the publication of *Blitz Requiem* in
Conductor's Score, Full Score, and Vocal Score.

Music copyright © David Goode 2013
Words copyright © Francis Warner 2013
Cover image: *St Paul's Survives* © Herbert Morrison
Associated Newspaper / Solo Syndication

Vocal Score: ISBN 978-0-86140-491-9
Full Score: ISBN 978-0-86140-492-6
Conductor's Score: ISBN 978-0-86140-490-2

Text prepared by Alison Wiblin
Designed by Libanus Press, Marlborough
Printed by Hampton Printing (Bristol) Ltd

The first performance of *Blitz Requiem* was given in St Paul's Cathedral,
London, on 26 September 2013.
The soloists were Emma Tring, Suzanna Spicer, Matthew Long and Robert Davies,
with the Bach Choir and the Royal Philharmonic Orchestra
(Leader Clio Gould) conducted by David Hill

Soprano, Mezzo-Soprano, Tenor, Baritone
SATB Chorus

2 Flutes (2nd doubling Piccolo); 2 Oboes (2nd doubling Cor Anglais);
2 Clarinets (2nd doubling Bass Clarinet); 2 Bassoons (2nd doubling Contra
Bassoon); 4 Horns; 2 Trumpets; 2 Tenor Trombones; Bass Trombone; Tuba;
Timpani; Percussion (Snare Drum, Bass Drum, Cymbals, Tubular Bells,
Tam-tam, Triangle); Harp; Organ; Strings

Duration: one hour

The première was broadcast on Classic FM.
It was generously sponsored by the Murphy Foundation,
with additional support from Victoria Sharp and Simon Yates.

DEDICATED
TO THOSE
WHO SAVED US

COMPOSER
DAVID GOODE

DAVID GOODE, M.A., M.PHIL., born 1971, composer and organist, combines a concert career that takes him round the world with being Organist of Eton College, where as a boy he was a music scholar, and where his work includes teaching composition. From Eton he became Organ Scholar at King's College, Cambridge, 1991–1994, winning a double First Class Degree in Music, and taking the M.Phil in Musicology; then Sub-Organist at Christ Church, Oxford, where he also tutored. While there he wrote his first piece, *Like as the Hart*, for the cathedral choir. He won the top prizes awarded at the 1997 St Albans Interpretation Competition, and the Recital Gold Medal at the 1998 Calgary Competition. From 2003–2005 he combined his busy international recital career with the post of Organist-in-Residence at First Congregational Church, Los Angeles, USA, home to the world's largest church organ. A frequent performer at the B.B.C. Promenade Concerts, where he has been a Featured Artist, he has made many recordings.

His compositions include work for the Los Angeles Philharmonic Orchestra, and his *Concert Fantasy on Themes by Gershwin* written for the new organ of Symphony Hall, Birmingham. His collaboration with Francis Warner began in 2004 when the choir of King's College, Cambridge, performed their *Anthem for St Cecilia's Day*; that partnership now numbers six anthems, all recorded by the choir of King's, a carol and a set of organ variations, all variously performed in Oxford, Cambridge, Eton and elsewhere. *Blitz Requiem* represents the culmination of this collaboration.

© Graham Keutenius

LIBRETTIST
FRANCIS WARNER

FRANCIS WARNER, M.A., D.LITT., HON. D.MUS., born 1937, is Emeritus Fellow of St Peter's College, Oxford, and Residential Honorary Fellow of St Catharine's College, Cambridge, where in the 1950s he was a Choral Exhibitioner and subsequently taught before moving to St Peter's in 1965. He divides his time between these two colleges.

After six years of war, five under the 1940–41 Blitz and subsequent Nazi bombardments, he was educated at Christ's Hospital and the London College of Music. At Cambridge he conducted his own re-scoring of Honegger's *King David* in King's College Chapel for two performances in 1958. In 2003 the recording of this concert was re-issued as a Landmark Recording CD by OxRecs Digital (OXCD-94).

Francis Warner's published works include sixteen plays, *Collected Poems 1960–1984*, *Nightingales: Poems 1985–1996*, *By the Cam and the Isis 1954–2000* (two long poems), and *Six Anthems* by David Goode and Francis Warner (issued with accompanying CD of King's College Choir, Cambridge, under Stephen Cleobury singing all six anthems in their liturgical context). His most recent publication is *Beauty for Ashes*, (2012, 2nd edition 2013) which includes *Blitz Requiem*, and *Armageddon and Faith*, Warner's *Commemorative Lecture for the seventieth anniversary of the Blitz* for Cambridge University, together with six of his war sonnets. It is issued with a CD: *Francis Warner as Musician in Performance*. All are published by Colin Smythe Ltd.

© Billett Potter

WORDS BY FRANCIS WARNER

The Second World War lasted nearly six years. From 8th August until 31st October 1940 the Royal Air Force and the Luftwaffe could be seen daily by everyone, spiralling above us killing each other.

Overlapping, from 7th September began the night Blitz concentrated on London for fifty-seven consecutive sunsets until the All Clear sounded at four or five in the morning.

From the following May, 1941, the Blitz became intermittent. During my first term at school, on the radio-beamed Nazi flight path over us from Cherbourg to London, Petworth Boys' School to the south-west of my home was bombed in a daylight raid, killing the Headmaster and thirty-two others, boys and staff. During my second term Sandhurst Road School, Catford, only a flying minute or two beyond us to the north-east, was machine-gunned and bombed leaving thirty-one children and six members of staff laid out dead on the playground. A further seven children died later in hospital. My younger brother, Martin, was born under the dining room table during one of the heaviest bombing raids of the war. Afterwards came the flying bombs —'doodlebugs' we called them — and then during the final year of the war the terrifying V2 rockets, against which we had no defence.

Blitz Requiem draws on my childhood experiences of five years under these conditions, and uses the framework of the traditional Latin Mass to come to terms with what I, my three brothers and baby sister, chose to suppress as we agreed to look forward, not back. This work renders the Requiem wholly in English, (though with echoes of the original verse forms) as it speaks for the 'ordinary, decent citizens'. It came about because Cambridge University invited me to give a lecture commemorating the seventieth anniversary of the Blitz. This poem is the distillation of my reluctant re-visiting of those childhood years of which the detailed memories turn out not to have faded at all.

MUSIC BY DAVID GOODE

The music for *Blitz Requiem* was begun in December 2011, and written on and off around other projects for nearly a year and a half. Throughout, the structure of Francis' poem, and the vividness of his verse, was the stimulus for the music that resulted.

The totemic sound of the Blitz is the air raid warning, a glissando in minor thirds, here synthesized at the very beginning on trombones and strings, and eventually crystallizing into chordal harmony. Much of the material of the piece is therefore derived from combinations of thirds, built up into chords or used melodically. The harmonic style is late-Romantic to modern, somewhat impressionistic, part of the English choral tradition, to be sure; but (one hopes) something of itself.

The *Requiem* movement appears three times in the work, related but altered each time. The mood here is luminous and atmospheric. *Requiem I* leads without a break into the *Absolve and Kyrie*. Here the soloists inhabit grittier landscapes, and are given more angular music to sing (accompanied by leaner orchestration). This is contrasted and interleaved with the incantatory lines of the Greek *Kyrie*, intoned in three groups of three by the chorus.

Dies Irae is the longest movement, a vivid drama lasting some 17 minutes. Each section of this is based, motivically, on a line of the *Coventry Carol*, the mediaeval carol in which Herod's Massacre of the Innocents is bemoaned. The parallels with the scenario described could hardly be clearer. Martial rhythms on the side drum introduce the opening storm, which presently subsides into three arias: darkly expressive for the alto, more pastoral (though not without its own drama) for the tenor; and for the bass a series of declamations set against hushed choral responses. The opening material returns, building to the whole work's central catastrophe: 'blast'. Out of this the soprano, counterpointed with the bird-like tones of the piccolo, sings in ethereal tones of 'dawn's peaceful olive', now 'blasted'. A solo trumpet intones fragments of the *Coventry Carol*, heard plainly at last. Hushed horror turns to a more affirmative, purposeful mood at 'Shall these children be forgotten?'; but the movement ends darkly, with the ominous layers of *ostinati* for 'Armageddon'.

The *Sanctus* offers a respite from such sombreness. The chains of thirds become a lilting 'minimalist' texture of shifting patterns, set in F major, as though of dappled sunlight, over which the chorus spin more expansive lines, leading to a radiant climax at 'Creator of the world'. A brief *Benedictus* follows at 'We bend', with a momentary reprise of the opening to conclude.

Grave moods return with *Agnus Dei*, set in D minor. The rhythms of the Latin text are invoked by the expressively angular lines of the *cor anglais* melody, soon counterpointed by that of the alto soloist. The lower voices of the choir form a solemn backdrop to the alto's lament. For the last line of text, 'May we arise with you in ecstasy', we move to D major with a conscious echo of the cathartic resignation of Mahler's *9th Symphony*.

The *Responsorium*, an aria for bass solo and orchestra, takes the form of a *passacaglia* in G minor, the 'darkest' key of the piece. Bassoons and strings successively add their counterpoints, and at the fourth repetition the voice enters. Soon the theme moves up through the texture, rising also harmonically by a fifth each time. As the voice receives it ('this violent hour') we are in B minor; then F sharp minor, the furthest remove; then we crash into G minor for a *tutti* conclusion. Here, a potent model is perhaps Frank Martin's fine *Passacaille* for organ, written in 1944.

The violins lead us down from this highly charged mood to a modified return of the *Requiem* music, by now almost forgotten. There follows *In Paradisum*, whose text presents a darker conception than might be expected from the title. At 'Cry out' the mood therefore quickly returns to that of the *Dies Irae*, with ominous rumblings beneath a high solo violin; and the soloists then return to the style of *Absolve and Kyrie* with short declamatory phrases, shadowed (as in *Agnus Dei*) by *ostinati* from the chorus. The intensity builds to an ecstatic climax at 'May angels', fading into the clouds.

The final *Requiem* movement follows without a break. 'On these may light' is expanded; radiant chords appear for 'Shine and deliver'; and the orchestra gradually reduce the chains of thirds back to the opening *glissando* of the whole piece. We end however with only rising *glissandi*, the sound of the 'All Clear'; thus the piece ends in the major key of A, with hope arising out of suffering as surely as the dome of St Paul's rose from the clouds of the Blitz.

BLITZ REQUIEM

REQUIEM AETERNAM

May souls in peace rest beyond reach of time,
Healed from the horror of their parting hence.
On these may light perpetual, sublime,
Shine and deliver from all past offence.

ABSOLVE AND KYRIE

Deliver us from menace in the dust,
Long hours in the cold waters of the sea,
The failing parachute, the bayonet thrust –
May we know our sin nailed you to the tree.

Lord have pity on us
Lord have pity on us
Lord have pity on us

For malice in revenge and cruel laugh
Teach us our own responsibility,
For those who now take life on our behalf,
Those who are dying so we may be free.

Christ have pity on us
Christ have pity on us
Christ have pity on us

From our indifference to consequence
Of our retaliation, make us pause.
Forgive us glorifying Judas' pence.
Christ, make ourselves more fit to serve your cause.

Lord have pity on us
Lord have pity on us
Lord have pity on us

DIES IRAE

What fresh terror sirens' moaning
Heralds? Earth and heaven groaning
At near raiders' engines' droning,

Night sky lit with flames ascending,
Wrath and fear in ashes blending
With each dive-bomber's descending.

Underneath a dining table
On a mattress, while the babel
Of a thousand aircraft able

To destroy a sleeping city
Streams above, a mother's pity
Rolls her in birth-agony.

From the dog-fight high in summer
Blue, where milk streaks spread in slumber,
And small boys look up in wonder

As one youth explodes in fire,
And another flying higher
Mushrooms down from funeral pyre;

From the flame-tailed rocket's rattle,
And the whine of bombs in battle
On civilians' lunch time prattle;

Packed between pews sleeping, church nights,
From the dark sky probed by searchlights,
Spare us further blinding eye sights.

Flying low with high explosive
Clearly aimed by creed corrosive,
Two eyes blast dawn's peaceful olive

On the playground; pencils scattered,
Homework, little things that mattered
Like these bodies, shrapnel–shattered

In school uniforms of cotton.
Trust in mass graves dead and rotten.
Shall these children be forgotten?

Lest our true compassion deaden
Let not hate make mercy leaden.
Spare us, Lord, in Armageddon.

SANCTUS

Almighty God whose goodness fills the height,
Creator of the world shielding our sight,
We bend our eyes down in your mercy's light.

AGNUS DEI

Good shepherd's dearest, dead in agony,
Our evil cleansed in perpetuity
May we arise with you in ecstasy.

RESPONSORIUM

In this red curse of combat, Lord, forgive
Each one of us who kill in hope to live –
Blind with tears. Your coming wrath must shake me
For what I do in fear. O Jesus, make me
Compassionate to captives in our power
In soul-scarred sins I choose this violent hour –
My shattering explosives leaping higher
Trembling me as you judge the world by fire.

REQUIEM AETERNAM

May souls in peace rest beyond reach of time,
Healed from the horror of their parting hence.
On these may light perpetual, sublime,
Shine and deliver from all past offence.

IN PARADISUM

May saints and martyrs in this extreme time
Cry out in anguished prayer for us above
As earth's foundations shake in shame and crime.
Crucified Jesus, pity in your love
The fireman struggling as forlorn hope dims,
Doctor and priest each doing all he could,
Nurses and teachers sorting out torn limbs,
Mothers and children digging to grow food
On their allotments with potatoes, hens;
Old journalists stumbling to find the facts –
The ordinary, decent citizens,
All of them blasted in unselfish acts:
Good people who have paid the highest price.
May angels lead them into Paradise.

REQUIEM AETERNAM

May souls in peace rest, beyond reach of time,
Healed from the horror of their parting hence.
On these may light perpetual, sublime,
Shine and deliver from all past offence.

FRANCIS WARNER
March 2011

REQUIEM I

Absolve and Kyrie

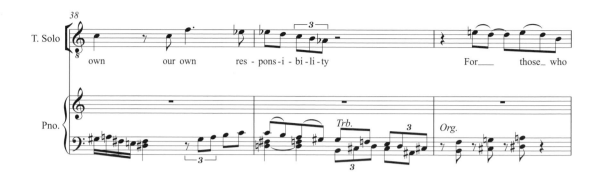

own our own res-pons-i-bi-li-ty For___ those_ who

now_____ take life on___ our be- half, Those_ who are dy-ing Those

___who are dy-ing that we may be free.

A. Christ___

T. Christ___ have pi-ty on us on

B. Christ___ have pi-ty on us on

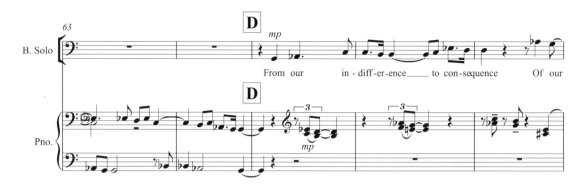

From our in-diff-er-ence____ to con-sequence Of our

____ re-ta-li-a - tion make us pause.____ For - give us glo - ri -

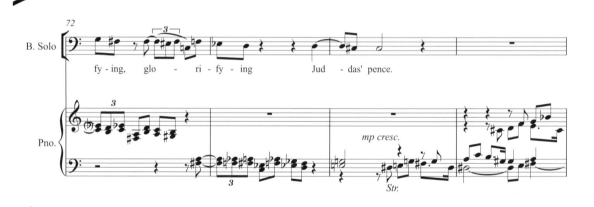

fy - ing, glo - ri - fy - ing Jud - das' pence.

Christ____ make our-selves more fit____ to serve your cause.

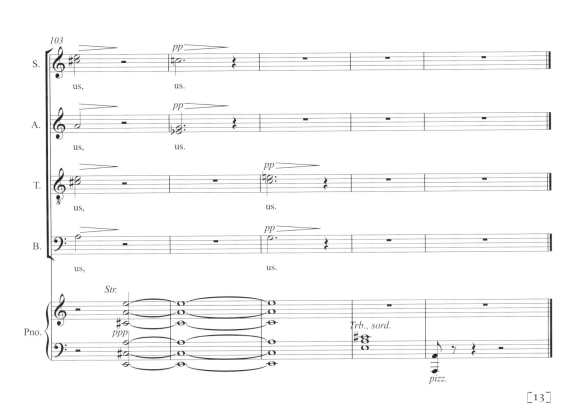

DIES IRAE

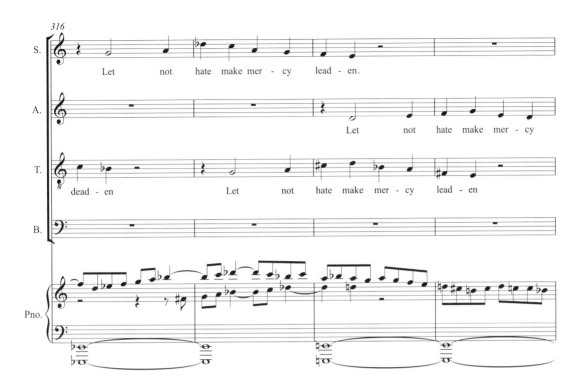

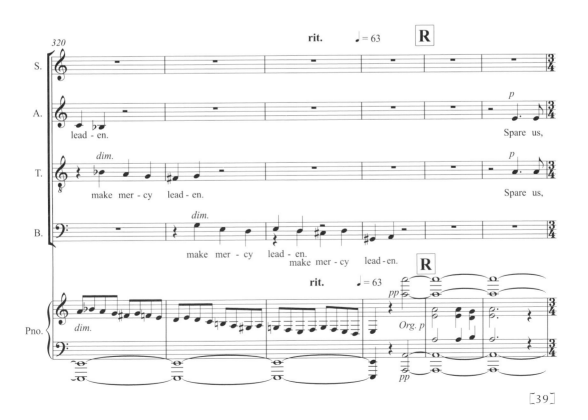

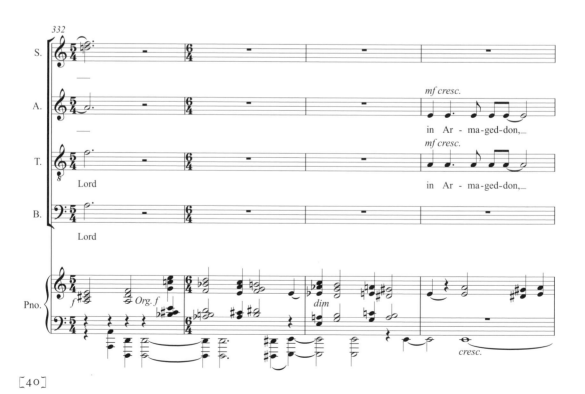

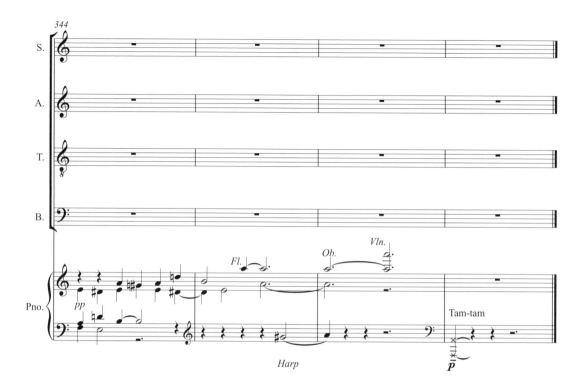

SANCTUS

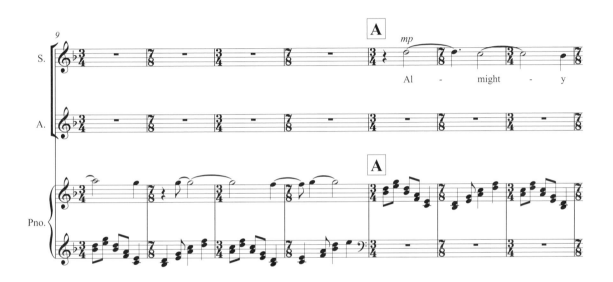

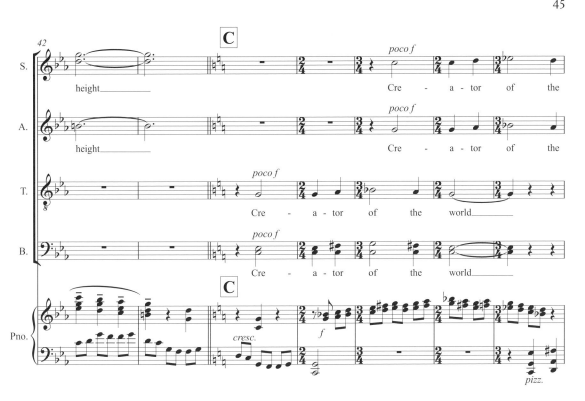

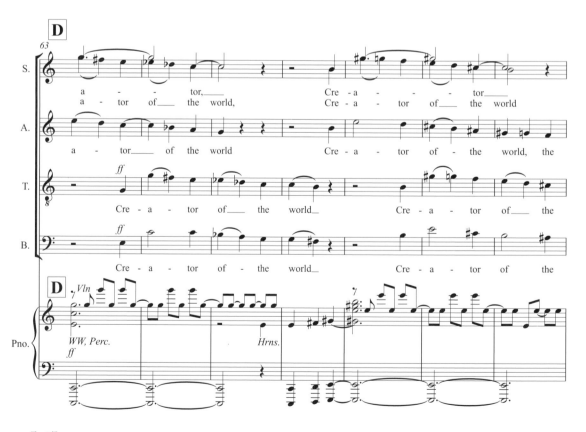

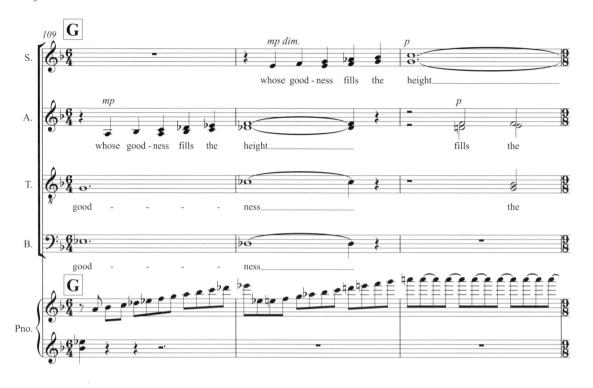

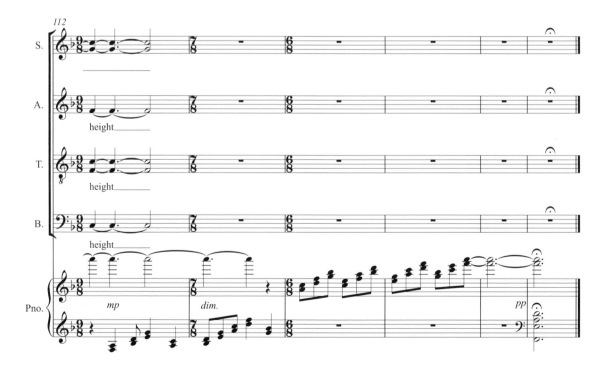

AGNUS DEI

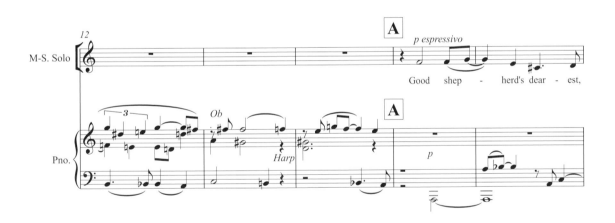

52

[52]

RESPONSORIUM

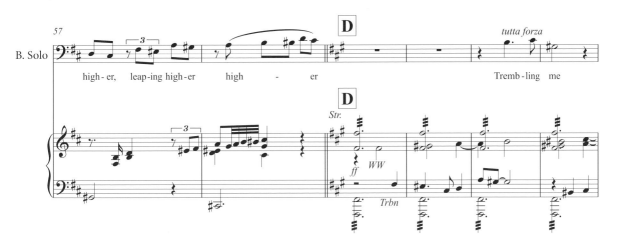

B. Solo

high-er, leap-ing high-er high - er Tremb-ling me

B. Solo

as you judge the world___ by fire.

REQUIEM II

IN PARADISUM

62

REQUIEM III

The photograph overleaf is by William Vandivert,
by kind permission of Susan Vandivert-Olin ©